Common Core Lessons & Activities:

Energy

By Carole Marsh

Published by Gallopade International, Inc.

Printed in the U.S.A. (Peachtree City, Georgia)

TABLE OF CONTENTS

G: Includes Graphic Organizer

GO: Graphic Organizer is also available 8½" x 11" online download at www.gallopade.com/client/go

(numbers above correspond to the graphic organizer numbers online)

MAIN IDEA

Energy from the Sun

Read the text and answer the questions.

The sun is not the only source of energy on Earth, but it is one of the most important. Without the sun's energy, life on Earth would not exist. Why is the sun so important? Much of the energy on Earth comes directly or indirectly from the sun.

Some energy on Earth comes directly from the sun. From about 93 million miles away, the sun's light energy and heat energy travel through space to the Earth. Without light and heat from the sun, Earth would be completely dark and frozen.

Some forms of energy on Earth are indirectly created by the sun's light and heat. For example, the energy stored in food starts with light from the sun. Through a special process, plants change the sun's energy into chemical energy they need to grow. Animals, as well as people, eat the plants as food. An animal's body changes the chemical energy from food into mechanical energy to move its muscles.

The sun's heat also indirectly creates energy on Earth. The sun's heat warms the planet and causes air to move. The movement of air heated by the sun creates cool and warm breezes. Wind can be used to make electricity for homes and businesses.

1. A. What is the main idea of this text?
   B. What details does the author use to support the main idea?

Use the text to classify each source of energy as being either **directly** or **indirectly** from the sun:

A. ____________ warmth on a sunny day
B. ____________ vegetables you eat as food
C. ____________ light outside in the daytime
D. ____________ light inside your house at night

2. Draw a simple diagram to show how the sun creates the food you eat.

3. A. Explain why the sun is important to life on Earth.
   B. Predict what would happen to life on Earth if only half of the sun's light reached Earth. Support your prediction with logical reasoning and evidence from the text.

Potential and Kinetic

Read the text, look at the diagrams, and answer the questions.

All forms of energy fall into two categories:

Potential energy is stored energy that is waiting to be set in motion. Potential energy exists because of the position of objects. For example, a rock at the top of a hill has potential energy that is released (as mechanical energy) when gravity causes the rock to fall. Firewood has potential energy that is released (as light and heat energy) when it is burned. Food has potential energy that is released (through a chemical reaction) when your body digests it. Atoms have potential energy that is released (through the movement of electrons) to produce electricity.

Kinetic energy is energy in motion. When potential energy is released, it turns into kinetic energy. Kinetic energy can be movement, light, sound, electricity, or even heat.

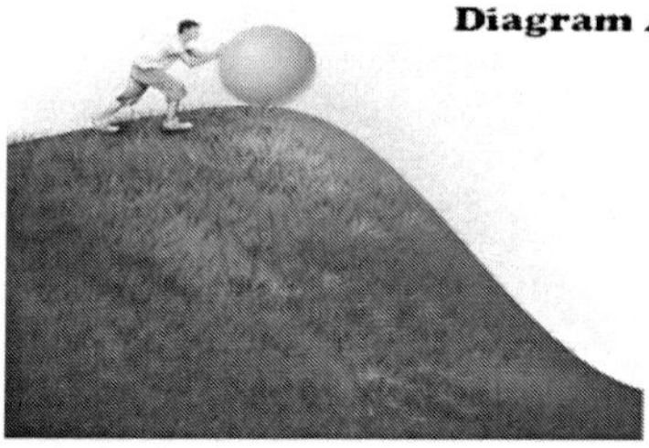

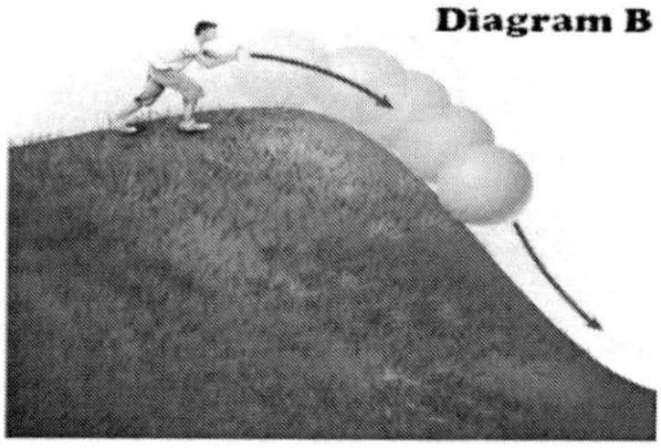

1. A. Use the text to define potential energy and kinetic energy.

2. A. Which diagram shows the ball with potential energy?
   B. Which diagram shows the ball with kinetic energy?
   C. What two forces caused energy to change forms?

3. Determine which part of each example is **potential energy** (**PE**) and which part is **kinetic energy** (**KE**):
   A. Wood (___) is burned to release light and heat (___).
   B. Light (___) is absorbed by a plant's leaves and stored as sugar and starch (___).
   C. A book (___) in your hand falls (___) to the ground.
   D. Energy from food (___) is used to move your muscles (___).
   E. Heat (___) is stored in the chemical bonds (___) of baked food.

Forms of Energy

Read the definitions and answer the questions.

Potential energy is stored energy. Kinetic energy is energy in motion. Some forms of energy are potential, some are kinetic, and some can be either.

Sound energy: energy produced by the vibration of an object. It moves as a wave. Your eardrum detects the sound wave and you hear sound.

Chemical energy: energy stored in molecules that can be released by a chemical reaction. It is stored in food, gasoline, and other substances.

Electrical energy: energy stored in the electrons of atoms and released when electrons move. We use it to produce light, movement, and more.

Light energy: electromagnetic radiation. Light energy is stored in particles called photons that move as a wave.

Thermal (heat) energy: energy stored in an object, as the object's temperature, that can be released as heat. It is caused by excited, fast-moving atoms.

Nuclear energy: energy stored in the atoms of all things, released by a nuclear reaction (splitting atoms in fusion or fission).

Mechanical energy: the potential energy stored in objects (including gravitational energy) and the kinetic energy of objects in motion.

1. A. Name two types of energy that move in waves.
   B. Name two organs in your body that detect these energy waves.
   C. Name the sense that each of these organs gives you.

2. Complete each sentence with the correct form(s) of energy:
   A. You can see the sun's ________ energy and feel its ________ energy.
   B. Some electrical power plants split atoms to release ________ energy.
   C. A light bulb uses ________ energy to produce ________ energy.
   D. To lift a box above your head, you need to use ________ energy.
   E. Food contains ________ energy your body uses to grow and move.
   F. A person who cannot hear is unable to detect ________ energy.

3. Create a table listing the 7 forms of energy in the text. Additionally, include the following information in the table for each energy form:
   A. Is it potential energy?
   B. Is it kinetic energy?
   C. Give an example of how each form of energy can be observed.

4. **True** or **False**: One form of energy can be transformed into another form of energy. Explain.

APPLYING CONCEPTS

Gravitational Energy

Read the text and answer the questions.

You might not notice gravity, but it affects you every moment of every day. Earth's gravity pulls all objects, including you, down toward the ground. Without gravity, objects on Earth would float off the ground and into space!

Because of gravity, objects above the ground have potential energy stored in them. Imagine you lift a textbook a foot above your desk. By lifting it, you have given the textbook gravitational energy. You let it go. What happens? It falls. Why? The pull of gravity causes the textbook to fall, changing the potential energy (stored) into kinetic energy (motion)!

The gravitational energy of an object depends on its mass (its matter, which is usually measured and described as an object's weight) and its height above the ground. Objects that have more mass (are heavier) have more gravitational energy. Objects that are higher above the ground have more gravitational energy, too.

1. A. Define gravitational energy as it is used in the text.
   B. What two factors affect the amount of gravitational energy stored in an object?
2. Describe the relationship between mass and weight.
3. Analyze the data in the table and add the missing information: For the first 2 examples, add a greater than (>) or less than (<)sign. For the last 2 examples, add an object or height above ground.

Object 1	Height above ground	Gravitational Energy > or <	Object 2	Height above ground
Boulder	10 Feet		Pebble	10 Feet
Penny	100 Feet		Penny	90 Feet
Brick	100 Feet	<		100 Feet
Apple		<	Apple	40 Feet

4. What happens to a falling object's gravitational energy as the object falls to the ground? Explain why.

EXPERIMENT ANALYSIS

Galileo's Experiment

Read the text and answer the questions.

Through most of the 1500s, many scientists thought gravity caused heavier objects (objects with more mass) to fall faster than lighter objects (objects with less mass). In 1589, the Italian scientist Galileo did not believe this, and he performed an experiment to try to prove this theory wrong.

Galileo got two metal balls, one heavy and one light. Then he and his students went to the leaning tower of Pisa, where Galileo had decided he would perform the experiment.

Galileo carried the balls to the top of the tower, while his students remained down below to observe. With great concentration, Galileo dropped the two balls at exactly the same time. Galileo's students on the ground carefully watched as the balls fell through the air.

The two balls hit the ground with a thud at the same time. Observers noted that the heavier ball made a deeper dent in the soft ground, but it did not fall any faster.

1. Place a ✓ next to the statement that best summarizes the purpose of Galileo's experiment.
   A) _____ To prove that gravity pulls objects to the ground.
   B) _____ To show that experiments are necessary to test new ideas.
   C) _____ To prove objects dropped from the same height fall at the same speed, regardless of mass.
2. List items you would need in order to recreate Galileo's experiment.
3. Write step-by-step instructions to perform the experiment.
4. List at least two likely reasons that explain why Galileo conducted his experiment in front of an audience.
5. A. Why did Galileo use two balls that had different weights?
   B. Why did Galileo drop the two balls at exactly the same time?
6. A. Write a hypothesis that reflects Galileo's point of view.
   B. Was Galileo's hypothesis shown to be correct or incorrect?

PRIMARY SOURCE ANALYSIS

Making an Impact

Read the text, look at the photographs, and answer the questions.

It takes energy to make something move. It takes more energy to move a heavier object than it takes to move a lighter one. If two objects are moving at the same speed, the heavier object has more energy than the lighter one. A moving object can transfer energy to another object by hitting, pushing, or pulling the other object.

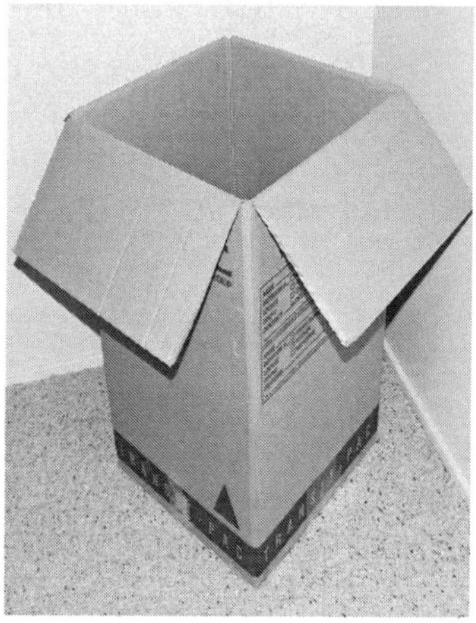

1. Compare and contrast the size, shape, weight, and composition (what it's made of) of the two objects in the photographs.
2. A. Which object would require the most energy in order to move it ten feet? Why?
   B. If both objects were rolling down a hill at the same speed, which object would have the most energy? Why? Where did the extra energy come from?
   C. If both objects were to hit another object, which object would transfer the most energy to the object that was hit? Why? Where did the extra energy come from?
3. Draw a diagram to show the flow of energy for each of the two objects based on the scenarios in A, B, and C, in the question above.

Mechanical Energy

Read the text and answer the questions.

Mechanical energy can be seen in the movement of an object as kinetic energy. Mechanical energy can be stored in an object as potential energy. Mechanical energy can be converted from kinetic to potential and back to kinetic with tension or compression.

Tension is created when an object is stretched. Tension is usually caused by a pulling motion. When an object is stretched and given tension, it tries to snap back into place. For example, if you stretch a rubber band, you give it tension. If you let go, the rubber band will snap back and release the tension.

Compression is created when an object is pressed together. Compression is usually caused by a pushing motion. When an object is compressed, it tries to expand back outward. For example, if you push in a spring, you give it compression. If you let go, the spring will expand and release the compression.

You use mechanical energy (your hand pulling or pressing) to add tension or compression to an object. Your mechanical energy turns into potential energy in the object. If you release the object, it snaps or springs back, turning its potential energy into kinetic energy of movement. This kinetic energy can even be transferred to another object, like when a spring-toy pops and flies into the air or when a pebble is shot using the rubber band in a slingshot.

1. Use the text to determine whether each word below describes **tension** (**T**) or **compression** (**C**).

   a) _____ pulled b) ____ pressed c) _____ expanded
   d) _____ stretched e) ____ pushed f) _____ squeezed

2. Look at illustrations A & B. For each illustration identify the type of energy shown (tension or compression), where energy comes from, where the energy transfers to, and when the energy changes from kinetic to potential and to kinetic again.

A.

B.

Chemical Energy

Read the text and answer the questions.

Chemical energy is a form of potential energy that is stored in the bonds between molecules of all objects. Everything has chemical energy stored in its molecules!

In a chemical reaction, molecules are combined or broken apart. Chemical energy is released from molecules as a result of the changes that occur in the chemical reaction. Chemical reactions can produce heat, electricity, motion, or other forms of energy. For example, if a chemical reaction causes an explosion, it will produce sound, light, heat, and mechanical energy (motion)!

One of the most common ways to cause a chemical reaction is by adding heat. For example, wood contains chemical energy that can be released with fire. But where does the released energy go? In the case of a fire, the wood's energy is changed into light energy, heat energy, and sound energy. In the chemical reaction that occurs when wood is burned, the only parts of the wood not changed into another form of energy are smoke particles and ashes.

All living things use chemical energy to get food so they can live and grow. Plants use a chemical process called photosynthesis to absorb light energy and change it into chemical energy they use as food. Animals convert the chemical energy in food they eat into mechanical energy so they can grow, move, breathe, and live, in the chemical reactions that occur during the process of digestion.

1. Match each of the following questions to whether they are best answered by paragraph 1, 2, 3, or 4 of the text.
   A. _____ What is the process that releases chemical energy?
   B. _____ What is chemical energy?
   C. _____ Why is chemical energy important to life on Earth?
   D. _____ What role does heat play in chemical reactions?

2. A. What is a chemical reaction?
   B. Describe the effects of a chemical reaction.

3. Draw a diagram of wood in a fire and label/describe each form of energy that is released in the chemical reaction.

4. Compare and contrast the processes of photosynthesis and digestion.

PRIMARY SOURCE ANALYSIS

Nutrition

Look at the label and answer the questions.

Sample label for Macaroni & Cheese

(1) **Start Here**

(2) **Check Calories**

(3) **Limit these Nutrients**

(4) **Get Enough of these Nutrients**

(5) **Footnote**

Nutrition Facts

Serving Size 1 cup (228g)
Servings Per Container 2

Amount Per Serving

Calories 250	Calories from Fat 110
	% Daily Value*
Total Fat 12g	**18%**
Saturated Fat 3g	**15%**
Trans Fat 3g	
Cholesterol 30mg	**10%**
Sodium 470mg	**20%**
Total Carbohydrate 31g	**10%**
Dietary Fiber 0g	**0%**
Sugars 5g	
Protein 5g	
Vitamin A	4%
Vitamin C	2%
Calcium	20%
Iron	4%

* Percent Daily Values are based on a 2,000 calorie diet. Your Daily Values may be higher or lower depending on your calorie needs.

	Calories	2,000	2,500
Total Fat	Less than	65g	80g
Sat Fat	Less than	20g	25g
Cholesterol	Less than	300mg	300mg
Sodium	Less than	2,400mg	2,400mg
Total Carbohydrate		300g	375g
Dietary Fiber		25g	30g

Nutrition Vocabulary

calorie — a measurement of the energy in food

daily value — the amount of calories or nutrients that a "typical" person needs each day

nutrient — a substance that is essential for life and growth

serving size — the quantity of food that is suitable for a person to eat; the other numbers on a food label are based on the serving size

1. A. How much potential energy is in one serving of this food item?
   B. How much potential energy is in the entire container?
2. How does the energy in this food turn into energy you can use? Describe how energy changes forms in this process.
3. How does whether you get 2000, 2500, or a different number of calories each day affect the amount of energy you get?
4. What happens if you eat more calories than the daily values are based on, but use less energy than the daily values are based on? Why? Name two ways to solve the problem this creates.
5. Almost all food sold in grocery stores includes a Nutrition Facts label similar to this one. List at least 3 ways this information is beneficial.

Forms of Energy

Complete the graphic organizer:

A) In the center box, define energy.

B) In the circles, illustrate each form of energy.

C) On the lines, explain how each form of energy can be used.

POTENTIAL ENERGY

Chemical

____

____

____

ENERGY

Definition

Nuclear

____

____

____

Mechanical

____

____

____

KINETIC ENERGY

Electrical

Light

Sound

Thermal

Mechanical

Generating Electricity

Read the text and answer the questions.

Method 1:	Method 2:
1) Water falls from a high place with great gravitational force. 2) The falling water hits and turns a turbine. 3) The turbine's motion rotates a magnet around wire in an electrical generator. 4) The generator produces electricity.	1) Coal is burned to create heat that causes water to boil and turn into steam. 2) The steam rises and turns a turbine. 3) The turbine's motion rotates a magnet around wire in an electrical generator. 4) The generator produces electricity.
Method 3:	**Method 4:**
1) A solar panel collects the sun's light to create heat that causes water to boil and turn into steam. 2) The steam rises and turns a turbine. 3) The turbine's motion rotates a magnet around wire in an electrical generator. 4) The generator produces electricity.	1) Atoms of plutonium are split in a nuclear fission reactor, releasing heat energy that causes water to boil and turn into steam. 2) The steam rises and turns a turbine. 3) The turbine's motion rotates a magnet around wire in an electrical generator. 4) The generator produces electricity.

Mechanical energy: energy an object has due to its movement or position

Electrical energy: energy delivered or absorbed by an electrical current

1. For each Method in the text, determine the original source of energy, identify the source as kinetic energy or potential energy, and explain how its energy is used. Create a table to summarize this information.
2. A. What is the purpose of the turbine in each Method?
   B. What is the purpose of the generator in each Method?
3. A. How is the use of water similar in some Methods?
   B. How is the use of water different in some Methods?
4. Explain the relationship between mechanical energy and electric energy as described in the text.
5. Make inferences to determine which Method best fits each description below. Explain your reasoning for each choice.
   A. generates electricity fastest
   B. generates electricity slowest
   C. causes most pollution
   D. causes least pollution

Using Electricity

Read the text and answer the questions.

In the morning, Kathy wakes up to an alarm. She turns on the light next to the bed. The heater has been running all night, so she turns on the air conditioning. Kathy turns on the light in the bathroom and brushes her teeth with an electric toothbrush. After taking an hour-long shower with hot water from an electric water heater, Kathy dries her hair with an electric blow dryer.

Kathy's stomach rumbles—she is hungry. She turns on the kitchen light and gets a glass of milk out of the refrigerator. Kathy warms her toast in a toaster and turns on the television to watch the Saturday morning shows.

After breakfast, Kathy calls her friend Joe to come over. While she waits, she works on a school research project on her computer. When Joe arrives, Kathy prints out her notes, while the TV blares in the background. Then she and Joe head outside to ride bikes.

1. Complete the graphic organizer by identifying electrical devices in Kathy's home.

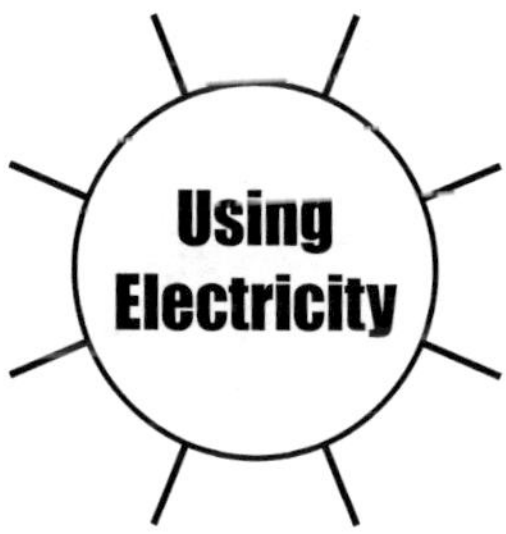

2. A. List at least three examples from the text to support the inference: "Kathy is not concerned about conserving electricity."
   B. For each example, suggest an alternative way that Kathy could conserve electricity.

Energy Sources

Read the text, look at the infographic, and answer the questions.

Renewable energy is energy that comes from natural resources that are not used up as they generate electricity, or that can be replaced in a relatively short time.

Non-renewable energy is energy that comes from natural resources that are used up as they generate electricity, and that cannot be replaced in a relatively short time.

Fuels are materials that are burned to produce energy. Fossil fuels (petroleum, natural gas, and coal) are fuels that took millions of years to form in the Earth. Biofuels are biomass materials—anything derived from plants or animals—that are burned to produce energy.

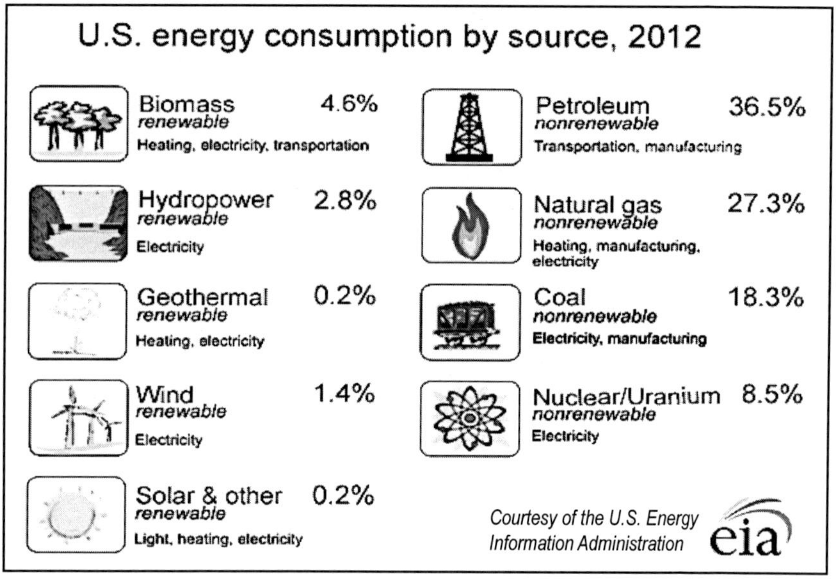

1. A. Who created the infographic?
   B. What types of information does the infographic provide?
   C. How is the information on the infographic organized?
   D. In your opinion, what is the purpose of the infographic? Explain why you think that.

2. A. What criteria is used to classify a resource as a renewable resource or as a nonrenewable resource?
   B. What can you infer about the process of using nuclear power to generate electricity? Explain your reasoning.
3. Identify whether each of the following items should be classified as biomass. Explain why or why not for each.
   A. trees
   B. water
   C. sunlight
   D. crops
   E. human waste
   F. garbage
4. Draw a circle graph to show how much of the U.S.'s energy consumption is from renewable resources and how much is from nonrenewable resources. Include a title, key, source, segment labels, and percents. You can approximate the size of the two segments.
5. Compare and contrast your circle graph with the infographic. Describe how they are similar or different in regards to:
   A. Detail of information provided
   B. Accuracy of information provided
   C. Effectiveness at communicating our energy source choices
   D. Effectiveness at communicating our energy source problems
6. Analyze the circle graph you created. Identify the "problem." Use the text, data, and logical thinking to complete the graphic organizer.

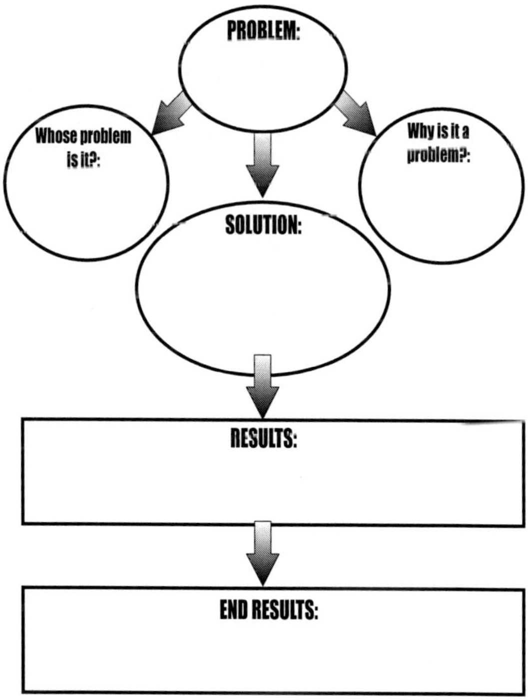

COMPARE & CONTRAST

Nuclear Energy

Read the text and answer the questions.

Coal power plants and nuclear power plants both produce electricity. However, their methods and results are different.

A coal power plant burns coal, causing a chemical reaction that releases energy. That energy is used to generate electricity. The process of burning coal is not too difficult, but it takes a lot of coal to generate the energy a coal power plant requires. And, coal is a non-renewable natural resource.

A nuclear power plant causes a nuclear reaction that releases energy that is used to generate electricity. Nuclear energy is stored in the nuclear bonds of every atom. When the nuclear bonds of an atom are broken, a great amount of heat energy is released. This process is more difficult than burning coal because nuclear energy can only be released under extreme heat. Nuclear power plants typically use uranium or plutonium as their fuel for producing electricity. Like coal, uranium and plutonium are non-renewable natural resources. However, one kilogram of uranium can produce the same amount of energy as nearly 15,000 kilograms of coal!

Coal power stations produce a tremendous amount of air pollution. When burned, coal releases carbon dioxide, which is thought to increase global warming of the Earth's atmosphere. In contrast, nuclear power stations produce almost no air pollution. However, nuclear power plants produce small amounts of nuclear radioactive waste. This waste is harmful to people, plants, and animals if not properly contained.

1. A. What is nuclear energy?
   B. How is nuclear energy released?

2. Complete the Venn diagram by comparing and contrasting the use of coal power and nuclear power to produce electricity.

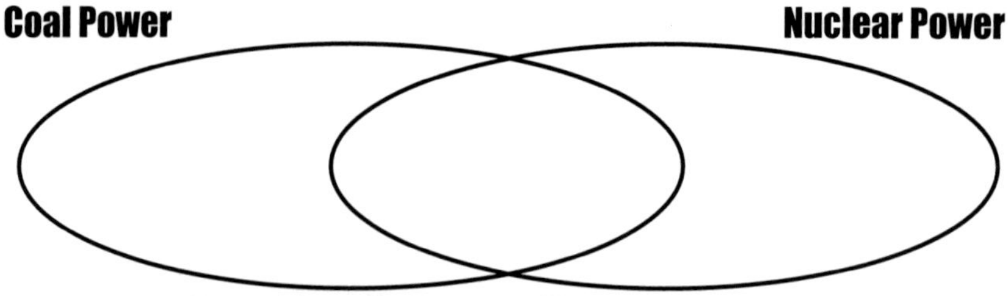

Nuclear Power

Read the quotations and answer the questions.

Quotation A

"For 50 years, nuclear power stations have produced three products only lunatics could want: bomb explosive plutonium, lethal radioactive waste, and electricity [at a high cost]."

–James Buchan, Scottish novelist

Quotation B

"Nuclear power will help provide the electricity that our growing economy needs without increasing [air pollution]. This is truly an environmentally responsible source of energy."

–Michael Burgess, U.S. Congressman

1. A. Compare and contrast the points of view of each quotation.
   B. What reasons does each author use to support his point of view?
2. Determine whether each quotation below supports the point of view of Quotation **A** or Quotation **B** above.
   A. _____ "All the waste in a year from a nuclear power plant can be stored under a desk."—*Ronald Reagan*
   B. _____ "The idea that the growing demand for energy worldwide can be met with energy from nuclear power is nonsense."—*Sigmar Gabriel*
   C. _____ "It's ridiculous that time and time again we need a radioactive cloud coming out of a nuclear power station to remind us that atomic energy is extraordinarily dangerous."—*Pierre Schaeffer*
   D. _____ "Nuclear power is an important part of our [country's] energy mix."—*Michael Burgess*
3. A. In your opinion, are the positive benefits of nuclear power worth the potential negative consequences? Why or why not?
   B. Debate this issue as a class.

EXPERIMENT ANALYSIS

Thermal Energy

Read the texts and answer the questions.

Thermal energy is what we call heat! It is caused by the movement of molecules. Hot substances have a lot of thermal energy, while cold substances have very little thermal energy.

EXPERIMENT

Procedure:

1. Place 3 beakers or glasses side by side on a table or counter.
2. Fill beaker 1 with room temperature water.
3. Fill beaker 2 with ice-cold water.
4. Fill beaker 3 with hot water.
5. Wait 1 minute for the water in each beaker to stop moving.
6. Add one drop of food coloring to each beaker and record your observations.

1. List all the items you will need in order to do this experiment.
2. Use the text to identify which beaker will contain:
   A. the **most** thermal energy B. the **least** thermal energy
3. Write a hypothesis for the experiment.
4. Under adult supervision, gather the materials listed and perform the experiment. Observe the movement of food coloring in each beaker and record your observations in the table.

Beaker 1	Beaker 2	Beaker 3

5. How did the temperature of the water affect the movement of molecules in the water?
6. Was your hypothesis correct? Write a conclusion that explains the relationship between thermal energy and molecule movement.

Sound

Read the text and answer the questions.

Sound is all around us. Sounds from televisions, radios, traffic, wind, animals, and machines bombard our senses. Sound can be quiet like a whisper, and sound can be loud like a yell. Some sounds are brief, like a beep, and some sounds are constant, like the gentle hum of an air conditioner. Sound can be pleasant, like the babbling of a stream or the purring of a cat. Sound can be sharp or alarming, too, like the crash of a breaking plate or the roar of thunder!

Where does sound come from?

First, something causes an object to vibrate. When an object vibrates, it transfers energy to the air in the form of sound waves. For example, when you pluck a guitar string, the string vibrates, releasing energy into the air in the form of sound waves. When you speak, your vocal chords vibrate, releasing energy into the air.

How do sound waves travel?

Sound travels in the form of a wave. As sound travels, it spreads out in all directions. The further sound travels from the source, the weaker the sound wave gets. In other words, the amplitude decreases as it travels.

How do we hear sound waves?

The human ear is very sensitive. When a sound wave travels into your ear, the wave's energy causes your eardrum to vibrate. You hear the vibrations as sound.

1. A. List at least five words used to describe sound in the text.
   B. List at least five other words you could use to describe sound.
2. Use the text to number the events in order.
   A. _____ Your friend slams the door.
   B. _____ You hear a loud noise.
   C. _____ Your eardrum vibrates.
   D. _____ Energy travels through the air as a sound wave.
   E. _____ The door slams shut, creating vibrations.
3. Explain why sounds that come from far away are more difficult to hear than sounds that are caused nearby.

Athletic Competition

Look at the photograph and answer the questions.

Courtesy of the Library of Congress

1. List 3-5 actions that occur in a basketball game that involve athletes using mechanical energy.
2. This photograph was taken just as the two athletes in the center of the photograph jumped up to shoot or block the basketball.
   A. Describe their kinetic mechanical energy.
   B. Describe their potential mechanical energy.
3. A. Where do athletes get the energy they use in a basketball game?
   B. What type of energy transformation occurs?
4. List and describe at least three other forms of energy (besides mechanical) that the athletes in this photograph are using. Cite evidence from the photograph to support each form you identify.

Changing Forms of Energy

Complete the graphic organizer by identifying and describing the energy transformation in each example.

Energy Form Before Transformation	Energy Form After Transformation	Description of Transformation Process
 Energy Form Before Transformation	 Energy Form After Transformation	Description of Transformation Process
 Energy Form Before Transformation	 Energy Form After Transformation	Description of Transformation Process
 Energy Form Before Transformation	 Energy Form After Transformation	Description of Transformation Process
 Energy Form Before Transformation	 Energy Form After Transformation	Description of Transformation Process
 Energy Form Before Transformation	 Energy Form After Transformation	Description of Transformation Process

Correlations to Common Core State Standards

For your convenience, correlations are listed page-by-page, and for the entire book!

This book is correlated to the Common Core State Standards for English Language Arts grades 3-8, and to Common Core State Standards for Literacy in History, Science, & Technological Subjects grades 6-8.

Correlations are highlighted in gray.

PAGE #	READING *Includes:* RI: Reading Informational Text RST: Reading Science & Technical Subjects	WRITING *Includes:* W: Writing WHST: Writing History/Social Studies, Science, & Technical Subjects	LANGUAGE *Includes:* L: Language LF: Language Foundational Skills	SPEAKING & LISTENING *Includes:* SL: Speaking & Listening
2	RI RST . **1** 2 **3** **4** **5** 6 7 **8** 9 **10**	W WHST . 1 **2** **3** **4** 5 6 7 **8** **9** **10**	L LF . 1 2 3 **4** 5 **6**	SL . 1 2 3 4 5 6
3	RI RST . **1** **2** **3** **4** **5** 6 7 **8** 9 **10**	W WHST . **1** **2** **3** **4** **5** 6 7 **8** **9** **10**	L LF . 1 2 3 **4** 5 **6**	SL . 1 2 3 4 5 6
4	RI RST . **1** 2 **3** **4** 5 6 **7** 8 **9** **10**	W WHST . 1 2 3 4 5 6 7 8 9 10	L LF . 1 2 3 **4** 5 **6**	SL . 1 2 3 4 5 6
5	RI RST . **1** **2** **3** **4** **5** 6 7 **8** 9 **10**	W WHST . 1 **2** 3 4 **5** 6 7 8 9 **10**	L LF . 1 2 3 **4** 5 **6**	SL . 1 2 3 4 5 6
6	RI RST . **1** 2 **3** **4** **5** 6 **7** **8** **9** **10**	W WHST . 1 **2** 3 **4** 5 6 7 8 **9** **10**	L LF . 1 2 3 **4** 5 **6**	SL . 1 2 3 4 5 6
7	RI RST . **1** **2** **3** 4 **5** **6** 7 **8** 9 **10**	W WHST . 1 **2** 3 **4** **5** 6 7 **8** **9** **10**	L LF . 1 2 3 4 5 6	SL . 1 2 3 4 5 6
8	RI RST . 1 2 **3** **4** **5** 6 **7** 8 **9** **10**	W WHST . 1 **2** **3** **4** 5 6 7 8 **9** **10**	L LF . 1 2 3 **4** **5** **6**	SL . 1 2 3 4 5 6
9	RI RST . **1** 2 **3** **4** **5** 6 **7** 8 **9** **10**	W WHST . 1 **2** 3 **4** 5 6 7 8 9 **10**	L LF . 1 2 3 **4** **5** **6**	SL . 1 2 3 4 5 6
10	RI RST . **1** **2** **3** **4** **5** 6 7 **8** 9 **10**	W WHST . 1 **2** 3 **4** 5 6 7 8 **9** **10**	L LF . 1 2 3 **4** 5 **6**	SL . 1 2 3 4 5 6
11	RI RST . **1** **2** **3** **4** 5 6 **7** 8 9 **10**	W WHST . 1 2 3 4 5 6 7 8 9 10	L LF . 1 2 3 **4** 5 **6**	SL . 1 2 3 4 5 6
12-13	RI RST . 1 **2** **3** **4** 5 6 7 8 **9** **10**	W WHST . 1 **2** 3 **4** 5 6 **7** **8** 9 **10**	L LF . 1 2 3 **4** 5 **6**	SL . 1 2 3 4 5 6
14	RI RST . **1** **2** **3** **4** 5 **6** **7** 8 **9** **10**	W WHST . 1 **2** 3 **4** 5 6 7 **8** **9** **10**	L LF . 1 2 3 **4** 5 **6**	SL . 1 2 3 4 5 6
15	RI RST . **1** **2** **3** 4 5 6 7 **8** 9 **10**	W WHST . 1 **2** 3 4 5 6 7 **8** **9** **10**	L LF . 1 2 3 4 5 6	SL . 1 2 3 4 5 6
16-17	RI RST . **1** **2** **3** **4** **5** **6** **7** **8** **9** **10**	W WHST . 1 **2** 3 **4** 5 6 **7** **8** **9** **10**	L LF . 1 2 **3** **4** **5** **6**	SL . 1 2 3 4 5 6
18	RI RST . **1** **2** **3** **4** **5** 6 7 8 9 **10**	W WHST . 1 2 3 4 5 6 7 8 9 10	L LF . 1 2 3 **4** 5 **6**	SL . 1 2 3 4 5 6
19	RI RST . **1** **2** **3** 4 5 **6** 7 **8** **9** **10**	W WHST . **1** **2** 3 **4** 5 6 7 **8** **9** **10**	L LF . 1 2 3 4 5 6	SL . **1** **2** 3 4 5 **6**
20	RI RST . **1** 2 **3** 4 **5** 6 **7** 8 **9** **10**	W WHST . 1 **2** 3 **4** **5** **6** **7** 8 **9** **10**	L LF . 1 2 3 4 5 6	SL . 1 2 3 4 5 6
21	RI RST . **1** **2** **3** **4** **5** 6 7 **8** 9 **10**	W WHST . 1 **2** **3** **4** 5 6 7 **8** **9** **10**	L LF . 1 2 3 4 5 6	SL . 1 2 3 4 5 6
22	RI RST . **1** **2** **3** **4** 5 6 **7** 8 9 **10**	W WHST . 1 **2** **3** **4** 5 6 7 **8** 9 **10**	L LF . 1 2 3 **4** **5** **6**	SL . 1 2 3 4 5 6
23	RI RST . 1 2 **3** 4 5 6 **7** 8 **9** **10**	W WHST . 1 **2** 3 **4** 5 6 7 **8** **9** **10**	L LF . 1 2 3 **4** 5 **6**	SL . 1 2 3 4 5 6
COMPLETE BOOK	RI RST . **1** **2** **3** **4** **5** **6** **7** **8** **9** **10**	W WHST . **1** **2** **3** **4** **5** **6** **7** **8** **9** **10**	L LF . 1 **2** **3** **4** **5** **6**	SL . **1** **2** 3 4 5 **6**

For the complete Common Core standard identifier, combine your grade + "." + letter code above + "." + number code above.

In addition to the correlations indicated here, the activities may be adapted or expanded to align to additional standards and to meet the diverse needs of your unique students!